converse

for
men

and
curious WOMEN

Jason Maverick

First published in Great Britain 2011 by Electric Press
info@electricpress.co

Comic Verse for Men and Curious Women
ISBN: 978-0-9568979-0-9
Copyright: ©Jason Maverick 2011

Illustrations: Nick Ash – *Alan the stunt tortoise, Amoeba, Einstein, It's not easy being a banana, Javelins and worms, John Prescott's secret life,* **and** *Weighing a fox*

John Random – *Proud to be Welsh* **and** *Whale song blues*

Sheba Cassini – *Teapot Collector*

Photography: Sylwia Kaczmarek

Design: Electric Press

Many thanks to:

My friend Cathryn Jiggens
for persuading me to get this book published.

My back injury
for giving me plenty of time staring at the ceiling
with a head full of surreal thoughts.

Dad for chuckling like a schoolboy at
"I'm turning into my dad."

And for my friends who gave me wonderful words
of encouragement, such as,
"Are you sure you don't take drugs?"

Enjoy!

Foreword

Born in Cardiff 1963, Jason spent his first 10 years
acting like a child.

As a teenager he channelled his obsessive tendencies into sport,
representing Wales firstly in athletics then subsequently in body
building. Unfortunately this has led to him finding it difficult
to throw away his speedos.

For someone with no singing ability his decision to become
lead singer for local punk band '*Exit the Monk*' seemed entirely
appropriate. He changed the band's lyrics from nihilistic
anti-establishment rants to joyful songs about worms.

In 1988 he ran away to mime school in London.
After a quiet year he began performing his mime and juggling
show around the world, and in 2001 was awarded 1st prize in the
prestigious Rotterdam International Street Theatre Competition.
This coincided with two years as a television presenter for
Channel 5's '*Havakazoo*', resulting in his creative juices
drivelling out verbally.

Jason performed for Her Majesty the Queen at her Golden Jubilee
party and will probably name drop for the rest of his career.

A passion for manipulating, twisting and toying with
the written word has resulted in his first book,
'Comic Verse for Men (*and Curious Women*)**'**.

Watch out for the sequel…
'Comic Verse for Kids'.

Contents

Recipe for water

Tried to make water today
Two spoons of hydrogen
One spoon of oxygen

It worked

But to be honest
I think I made it
a bit too runny

Brontosaurus

Brontosaurus

You were here before us

You were herbivorous

It's not easy being a banana

It's not easy being a banana
But it's all I know
No-one explained that curvature of the spine
is fine for me

It's not easy being a banana
With a fear of heights
from having skin
too thin to take a fall
without appalling bruises

It's not easy being a banana
A simple carbohydrate
yet complex in so many ways

It's not easy being a banana
Still,
It's better than being a satsuma

Naked politicians

Politicians
Cast aside your pretensions
Your personas
Your nationalistic masks
Your prejudices
Cast aside your clothes
Laugh with each other
Dance with each other
Hug
Fight
Anything
But be naked, be real

Come out of the shadows
of your image stylists
Cast aside your spin doctors
Be naked with your thoughts
Be naked with each other
Let's see Tony Blair in the buff
Let's see Anne Widdecombe's muff
Let's see Bush's spotty arse
Let's end the farce of projecting the person
you want us to see

Don't just pretend to be PC
to win elections
Show us your potency
Your intellectual erections
or just show us your erections
How liberating that would be

Let's have a naturist world summit
A nude United Nations
with delegations of world leaders
laying down their arms
full of Armani suits

Just stop talking bollocks
Stop fannying about
Be all the things you said you'd be
Don't just dress up words to impress us

Be naked, be real
Show us your ablutions
Show us some solutions that aren't clothed
in self interest

Let's have a naturist Houses of Parliament
and verbal volleyball
And let's all vote for
gritty
frisky
risk-taking
passionate
totally naked
politicians

A whole different gender

As I snuggle down
As I surrender to the ebbing final moments
of the day
As I am engulfed by soporific waves
As I tip-toe across the metaphorical bridge
between consciousness
and unconsciousness
At that moment
Yes
At that precise moment
…she wants to discuss our relationship

Women

They're like a whole different gender!

Facebook addict

I'm jubilant
I'm elated
My ego satiated
My desires lubricated
now my status has been updated
to...

"...ate sandwich for lunch"

Awaiting a reply
Now a craving
Can't deny
my day has gone awry
So please friends
Gratify me
Satisfy me
Whilst I'm checking and re-checking
Checking and re-checking

Ah...
Sweet surprise!
Two replies!

"Cheese?" says one
"Ham?" says the other

And so ends
another
beautiful day
on Facebook

Insomnia

I've developed insomnia
A worrying problem
but not worth
losing sleep over

I am a superhero

I am Superman
I am Don Juan
I am the Universal Lover
like no other

But she sees me
in my superhero tights
encased in kryptonite

Not quite
the perfection
I see in my own reflection
My S is slightly torn
My kiss curl, forlorn

Yet
I am a superhero

I am
The Invisible Man

But she
can see
right through me

The checkout girl knows

Out shopping
I mingle
amongst the crowd

No-one knows
I'm single
except the checkout girl

"Meal for one"
she says out loud

There's no surprise
No sympathy in her eyes
Just a look to say
she knows why
I'm single
I try to mingle
back in with the crowd
But a sign is flashing
above my head

'Single'

it says

'Probably no good in bed'

Hurrah the postman's arrived

Letters plop plopping
through the letterbox
My ears pricking up
like a frisky cocker spaniel

Tongue out

Salivating

Anticipating
perfume-scented letters
scattered across the floor
But finding
a postcard
addressed to the grumpy bloke
next door
and assorted
half-price price pizza leaflets
I return to the sofa
floppy eared
tail between my legs
And order a quattro formaggi pizza
…with extra cheese

Javelins and worms

Olympic javelin competition
Strength and technique
enveloped by Greek history
Watch in awe
as lethal weapons soar
through the air...

But spare a thought
for the poor family of worms
having a cozy night in
discussing home improvements

The javelin hurtles toward the 80 metre mark
Pierces the underground darkness
and pins father worm to his earthy bed

One man wins.
One worm dead.

At the medal ceremony
the athletes wear very, very thin
black armbands

Less pretty

Today you look less pretty
Your spark has gone
You don't stand out from the crowd
You are no longer the leading lady
Just another extra
in the film of my life
That potential wife label has disappeared
Today I've come to realise all your faults
because yesterday
you chucked me

Supermarket lust

We both reached up for a crusty roll
I gazed into your eyes
If I was the flour
then you were the yeast
and my baguette
it began to rise

Your hand touched mine by the current buns
The excitement was too much to take
'Cos you were my fruit fancy
The icing on my cake

Our temperatures rose
by the frozen food
where mutual lust now lingers
My body heat melts your frozen peas
and my bird eye fish fingers

You changed your mind whilst choosing desert
and lust turned to ridicule
I longed to be your chocolate fudge cake
but instead was a strawberry fool

My libido was finished
My ego diminished
My confidence began to deflate
My allure had subsided
for you had decided
I was past my sell by date

Turning into my dad

I'm turning into my dad
Collecting quirky personality traits
like ornamental pots
for the allotment
of my later life

I'm turning into my dad
My eyebrows are sprouting in all directions
My nasal hairs are having erections
which protrude down to my upper lip
My age is making me less hip
with the kids in the street
I'm leaving hip hop
for a future hip operation
And joining the generation who despair
at the indignation of youth

I'm turning into my dad
My face is metamorphosising into his
There's no disguising
my hairline has retreated to the top of my head
My hairdresser thinks I'm dead
it's been so long

I'm turning into my dad
My days at home are revolving
around endless cups of tea
The sound of the kettle symbolising
Earl Grey as my drug of choice

I'm turning into my dad
I feel like running, screaming,
tearing out the last remaining hairs
But in moments of still
reflection, you know what...
Turning into my dad
is not so bad after all

Now turning into my mother...
That's scary.

Anti-fashion

Distressed jeans,
they distress me
Fashionable,
yet unfathomable
Why pay for something ripped and torn
Time exposes thread-bare ideas
Once fashionable,
your woollen tank top lies crushed
physically and emotionally
in the bottom drawer
with the rest of the unloved

Weighing a fox

Weighing a fox
is usually easier
than weighing a whale
because foxes
can stand up on scales
but whales
just slip and fall off

Swimming against the tide

To Dave it seemed the world was obsessed
with the quest for losing weight
But Dave was skinny, very skinny
In the bath, his rubber duck would laugh
at his inadequate water displacement

Dave felt he was swimming against a tide
of low calorie soups
He was battling against a current of diet colas
in the river of life

Dave was salmonesque
Yet upstream
his office desk was awash with articles
about piling on the pounds
He longed to be round
but alas, his body was a monument to right angles
An animated X-ray
Attempting a smile when friends would say
"At least you don't have to worry about your weight"

His fate, he felt, was in his hands
He filled his fridge with the kind of foods
which were nails in the coffins
of the calorie conscious
Cholesterol-laden shelves beckoned
and Dave reckoned that his contentment lay within
He began gorging on globulous streaky bacon,
A dozen eggs, fried in lard so hard
it could block your arteries just by looking at it
All drizzled with enough Camembert cheese to please
a party of sumo wrestlers, at an all you can eat restaurant

Dave was elated,
Wiping grease from his face
he slumped in his chair
unaware,
that the food he was eating
was not regarded as cheating
on the Atkins diet
A tragic mistake
Skinny Dave lost weight
His paper thin lips released a sigh
He cried
Poor skinny Dave
Inside he knew a fat man was trying to get out

Sideboard

Bought a monogamy sideboard
Strange colour
and only my girlfriend
can open it

The apology

I wrote her a letter today
I tried to say
I'm sorry
I love you more and more
each day
But instead my pen broke free of my will
until my hand
couldn't stand it any more
Threw the pen to the floor
and a psychological war commenced
I sensed defeat
Dived under the seat
and retrieved the pen
But by then
my alter ego had mushroomed inside my head
and instead of words of devotion
my emotion had burst to the fore
and before I knew it
I blew it
and wrote
"It's all your bloody fault!"

Shoe fetish

My girlfriend has a shoe fetish
she leaves no sole unturned
No ankle boots are left unloved
no slingback shoes are spurned

A fortune spent on footwear
she keeps the cost concealed
My girlfriend has a shoe fetish
It's lucky she's well heeled

Amoeba

An amoeba
sitting in a petri dish
might wish for a more
fulfilling life
For holidays in the sun
Cuddles with his wife

But having no brain
he was content
…and spent
the rest of the day
being dissected

The problem with quantum mechanics

Damn
Left my cat
trapped
in the car
at the quantum mechanics garage
I phoned
They said
"There's a high probability it's alive

...or dead.

"You'd better come immediately"
I said
"I can't be in two places at once!"
They disagreed
I was exasperated
We deliberated
then berated each other
and had the mother of all arguments
which exploded from a singularity
and felt
unnecessary
considering
I only needed a new
headlight bulb

They said
"Light wave or particle version, mate"

Damn
these quantum mechanics
left me in a state
of confusion
And in conclusion
…I went to Kwik-Fit!

Pity the porpoise

Pity the porpoise
For the *'swimming with dolphins'* holidays
always grab the limelight
from the lesser known
'Paddling with porpoises'

The tortoise nudist beach

The tortoise nudist beach
is just out of sight
Just out of reach
of prying eyes

They slip out of their shells
just after sunrise
Small, wrinkled
blobs of flesh
basking in the sun
like prunes with legs

A wave crashes on the beach
Run tortoise run
But without shells
like overdone soufflés
they collapse in the middle
and are washed out to sea

Which explains the riddle
of why tortoises are seldom viewed
basking, shell-less
in the nude!

Poetry v cyber chat as a form of expression

I'd rather haiku
than tweet you

The afterlife awards

In the afterlife
will God line up
the Jews, Christians,
Hindus, Muslims, Sikhs
and announce the winner
of who was right?
I think she might be pretty diplomatic
and award everyone with runner up prizes

Two clowns go to war

Billy was a clown with a dark side
Blancmange quivered in his presence
Jelly wobbled
Raspberries rippled
And sausage rolls hurled themselves
onto cocktail sticks in a ritual suicide
His favourite trick was to take
birthday cake
out of the mouths of babes

Jo Jo however, brought happiness
His red noses glowed
His squirty flowers blossomed
His revolving wigs made him the Mr. Big
of children's parties

Then it happened
Showdown at the joke shop
…and it wasn't funny
Billy pulled out a gun
BANG said the letters
that unfurled
Jo Jo ran
Dodging a hail of rubber chickens

Billy pulled out his tickling stick
And with a few lunges and thrusts
he tickled Jo Jo to death
Flowers wilt
Make up runs
Head drops
Wig wobbles
Eyes close
Death
Billy leaves
Eyes open
Jo Jo giggles

Children dance
The sun shines
and laughter reigns
over everyone

Proof of the invalidity of quantum physics

I met a quantum physicist at a party
who assured me that
solid objects
never actually
come into contact with each other
So I threw a sausage roll
at his head
"Technically,' I said
"that never touched you!"

Unsuccessful polar expedition

Icy wind slapping my face
like cold steel
My fingers, solid, frozen together
like a chilled kit kat
only less chocolaty
Peephole eyes
peering out
at white forboding skies

Feet groaning at each torturous step
No sleep tonight
No respite
In the distance
a sign which signals defeat

Newcastle – two miles it says
In the street
locals pass by
wearing T-shirts
whispering *"soft southerner"* under their breath
I head south gorging on Kendal Mint Cake
as my dejected huskies shake their heads
with embarrassment

Sneaky plant

Plant
in my plant pot
There is not a lot
for you to do
nowhere to go

I think
your trying to grow
is a very slow way
of escaping

But ha ha!
I'm watching you
with my time lapse camera
You'll never get away

Proud to be Welsh

God I'm proud to be Welsh
The Seven Bridge
a symbolic gateway to heaven
The lushness of the grass
unsurpassed

The bewitching beauty of distant
undulating hills
The lilt in the voices
Cymru am Byth

My heart and mind rejoices
Wales forever!
I shout out loud
from my flat in Crystal Palace

Oil painting

You are no oil painting
You look slightly drawn
Your pigment is discoloured
Your features are more Picasso
than Rembrandt

Your canvas needs stretching
Your ageing frame
no longer requires touching up
But to me, you'll always be
a work of art

Holland

Holland;
to me you are inexplicably flat
At the dawn of your geological history
you lost the nerve
to ask for curves

Now you are a breeding ground for bicycles
They thrive on your flatness
Bask in your terrain

On a Sunday afternoon
bicycles could generate enough power
to turn your molehills
into mountains

But instead the tread of their wheels
just tickle you

Anemone

Two anemones were sitting on a rock one day
Both agreed 'anemone' was very hard to say
"Let's change our names," they said
"Quick, without delay!"
Now they're both called Bob
and they're happier that way
(Mind you, they sometimes forget
which one is which)

Looking for The One

Oxford Street
Saturday afternoon
A heaving jostling mass of humanity
Heads filled with thoughts of designer labels
and coffee shop rendezvous

Maybe she is amongst them
Not a female friend
Not a pretty woman who catches my eye
with her overly tight sweater
and milky thighs

But... *The One*

I mean
bloody hell
Can't she wear a sign or something?
Or a flashing neon light above her head
Can't she emit a high pitched sound
only detectable
by myself
and Chihuahuas?

I resort to standing
outside Oxford Street tube station
with a loud hailer
"Put your hand up if you're The One," I boom
I'm not quite sure if this will work
After all...
I don't want to appear desperate!

Personal ad

Male 36, Taurean
likes
Calligraphy
Remote-control helicopter flying
Nepalese cuisine
Lavatorial humour
Competitive arm wrestling
and
large breasts
Seeks female with similar interests

Attractive Female, 36
Deafened by the sound
of the biological clock ticking
Seeks male... with functional
genitals
Phone 24-hour hotline

Brief history of male underwear

My father wore underpants
on a grand scale
just below the chest
White cotton
Matching vest
Crotch sagging
like a wet nappy

Decades later
male genitalia
were less than happy
Figure hugging briefs
a fashion innovation
reaping genital havoc
causing scrotal suffocation
Until the cavalry arrived
in boxer shorts
and testicles everywhere
Sighed with relief
Jiggled in the street
Swung from side to side
and a few
like little hairy onions
just cried and cried
with happiness

Dalmatian fur

How does the fur of a dalmatian
know which dog to grow on?

If it made a mistake
a Rottweiler would not be pleased
Because
a Rottweiler with polkadots
would be teased
…from a distance.

Grrrrrr!

Changing the channel

The TV remote battery
is dying

I'm on my knees
trying to change the channel
a foot away from the screen

I won't give in

I won't be seen
touching the controls on the TV

I've paid for technology
and therefore
will remain
stubbornly
remote

Present for dad

Whatever I buy
However hard I try
Whatever present
presents itself
It is destined to return
to the same shelf
in the same shop
for a refund
or a straight swop

Years of frustration
Years of defeat
"Alright alright alright
dad
have the bloody receipt
Oh
and
Happy Birthday!"

Einstein

Einstein
revolutionised
our concept of time
He proved time runs
fast & slow
But sadly
he had
no time
to go...
for a haircut

She's getting ready

Steve and Natasha were going out

Steve put his shoes on

Natasha put on her moisturiser, foundation
Strawberry lip gloss, 2 for 1 blusher
Designer nails... with hearts on them
Push-up, push-in, push-out bra
Matching outfit
and her colour co-ordinated shoes

"Come on" said Steve

"Sainsbury's will be closed soon"

Low maintenance man

At 35
she is looking for something low maintenance
She finds him in a pub
One previous owner
Decent bodywork
Distinctive headlights
Sturdy enough to carry all her baggage
Keeps him well oiled
Temperamental gearstick though
Goes straight from first to fifth gear
Consults the manual
and re-adjusts her handling
Occasional inspection of undercarriage required
Takes him for a ride every Sunday morning
Low maintenance man
Full service history
Not required

Astrophysics

Out there in deep space
is a black hole
An extraordinary place
where matter is unimaginably dense
Light cannot escape
To me, this makes no sense

Sure enough,
one night
under cover of darkness
a little bit of light
escaped
whilst no-one was looking
Hawkings!
What does he know?

John Prescott's secret life

I'd like to discover
that John Prescott has a secret other life
as a lap dancer
in a seedy Soho bar
But has so far remained undiscovered
with the clever use of a blonde wig
and a very big
underwired bra

Builders and jeans

Jeans are not difficult
to wear correctly
Yet builders have trouble with the concept

Or is the exposure of the buttocks
A way of marking their territory

Or perhaps
a row of bum cheeks
are silently mouthing the words

"two sugars please"

In a glass frame

In a glass frame
in the hall
given prominence on the wall
was his last comb
Last used in September of '94
and near the door, a school photograph
Capturing the schoolboy laugh of the boy
blissfully unaware that
his unkempt hair and he
would part company
almost imperceptibly
and would disappear into the ether
slink into the sink unnoticed
Appearing briefly as a spidery mass
which with a last gasp
sunk without trace
Leaving a face with the look, of an open book
A page without edges
A field without hedges
A smile of recognition
of the transition of the stages
of the seven ages of man
All wrapped up succinctly
and distinctly by a phrase
Echoed throughout the days of his life
by his wife and friends
which transcends
each meeting with the greeting
"Alright baldy"

Motorway maintenance man

Oh motorway maintenance man
You live life in the fast lane
Spend night shifts in driving rain
whilst halogen lights illuminate your pain

You're a traffic jam catalyst
in need of an analyst

You were last seen
through my windscreen
Looking for a hard shoulder to cry on

Butternut squash

Oh butternut squash
What a beautiful surprise
When aged 35 I discovered
your sweet tenderness
I put you on a pedestal
as cabbages lay forlorn at your feet

Sorry swede; you just impede
my culinary style

Turnips; I turn up my nose at you

Broccoli; you are merely a cauliflower
with lowlights

But oh!
Butternut squash
mashed with a knob of butter!

Does life get any better than this?

My object of desire

She is more Apple Mac than PC
More iPhone than Blackberry

She is well sexy
And I have
an application
for her

Alan the stunt tortoise

You are stunt tortoise
Voles, rats and mice adore you
Turtles swim ashore to glimpse you
and your shiny shell

Love torn shrews promise fornication
Hamsters swoon in adulation
You are the city farm's new sensation
You are stunt tortoise

TV crews vie for your attention
Reptiles moisten
at the mention of your name
Your standing somersault led to global fame

Your lettuce is dipped in caviar
The paparazzi surround your car
You are a tortillian megastar
You are
The one and only
Stunt tortoise

Eh?

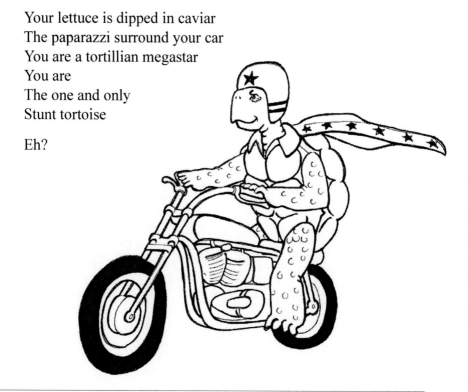

Molecular biology on the high street

In the summer
wearing short skirts and tight tops
women send off vibrations, ricocheting off walls

until all the molecules of nearby men
jostle together
… like schoolboys on a bus

Shhhh!

Sarah was a librarian
who took her work home with her
Not the books
The silence

She tip-toed from room to room
and loved nothing better
than a quiet night in

Once a month she went out
to a meditation class

One day I hid in the library
then leapt out in front of her
And screamed…

"*SARAH*!!!"

I really, really regret it now
But God, it was funny at the time

Rock climber

The rock climber was good
But would be better
if he was
a little bolder

Are you famous?

In my father's day
Celebrity meant
Hollywood glamour
Blockbuster movies
Sporting superstars
Untouchable, unreachable heroes
Whose mantle pieces glistened with awards

Today a celebrity
Is someone we've watched on TV
washing, eating and chatting on a sofa
Celebrities with nothing to celebrate
I hate them
Mind you
The other night they cooked potatoes
and that was quite interesting

Beauty salon for insects

Saturday morning, and the salon is full
Insects prepare for a night on the pull
Spiders in hairnets shout insults and grin
at slugs wearing mud packs for baby soft skin
Embarrassed stag beetles swallow their pride
and try to explore their feminine side
Grasshoppers leap to the front of the queue
their weekly knee massage is long overdue

Earwigs with highlights look strange but relaxed
whilst centipedes wait for their legs to be waxed
It costs them a fortune, so the staff all agree
they can have a bikini wax thrown in for free
Ants pick up magazines whilst they are waiting
read about bees who are hooked on speed dating
and how to become a much better lover
With canoodling cockroaches on the front cover
Stick insects on diets who think they're obese
learn insect anorexia is on the increase

The worm on reception
is having a moan
Without any limbs
she can't answer the phone
And gossiping wasps
whisper objections
to nearby flies
having Botox injections

It's Saturday teatime, the salon is closing
The manageress gives a look that's imposing
The air is then sprayed
with a pine fresh propellant
'Cos she's in love with the salon,
but finds insects repellant

Cheetah

Cheetah
Always in a rush

Take it easy
Relax
Take your foot off the gas

Your speed is impressive
but your emotional needs
are being left behind
in a cloud of dust

Don't burn yourself out
De-stress, chill out
Hang loose with the big cats

You are the fastest
but are you happy?

Look at the hyena
Shoddy runner
but always having a laugh

Whale song blues

Bought an album of whale song
Very relaxing, but not for the two whales
For their success in CD sales
Did not compensate
For the state of the recording studio
After they'd squeezed through the door

Karl Marx

Karl Marx was strongly political
His mind was analytical
But if you allow me to be critical
I'd say that
Although a classless society
might be inherently right
The revolutionary in me
would find it difficult to fight
for someone who on first sight
…looks like Father Christmas

Bus lane temptations

Oh bus lane
How you tempt me
So clog free
So clear
So near
And yet so far
from letting my car
caress your emptiness
in this rush hour queue

I implore you
Let me cruise down your gently parted thighs
that have materialised
like a vision before me

Avert those piercing camera eyes of yours
Let my wheels
and your tarmac combine

Let the two of us
entwine
Bus lane
I am yours
Be mine

Changing the duvet

In the wrestling ring
he is king
But in the bedroom
his duvet cover is kingsize
He tries to change it
They wrestle
And by his own admission
He loses by two falls and a submission

Imprint

Every thought you've had
Each experience
has left an imprint on your soul
Every kind word or deed
Every book you read
Every craving or need
has moulded you

Each potential mate
or disastrous date
has leapt off their pedestal & erected
barriers around you as a leaving present
Your imprints are unique
You are unique

So are you really surprised that
I don't bloody understand you

Very appropriate gifts

Two years together
He bought her
an egg timer
to take to the bathroom

She bought him
a patch
for his wandering eye

Hide and seek for scorpions

Scorpions don't often build sandcastles
but Nobby did

He went inside
and played hide and seek
with himself

He hid on a shelf
and found himself
one week later

"*Let's have another game,*" he said

"*Yes,*" he replied

"*this time... you hide*"

Tea pot collector

Pretty ones, cute ones
Quirky & minute ones
Tea pots, every one
in all shapes and sizes
Jazzy ones, plain ones
Fancy and mundane ones
and stupid little cupid ones
he won as fairground prizes

He loves them, treasures them
Takes them out and measures them
Names each and every one
Tea pots are his life
Wipes them and cleans them
Cherishes and preens them
Spends time with each of them
but sadly not his wife

Caresses them and dresses them
Puts tea cosy hats on them
Tea pots are No.1
Of this he has no doubt

Pottery and china ones
Porcelain designer ones
Tea pots are so much fun
but his wife is moving out

Tea pot collector man
Sad & dejected man
A newly rejected man
His marriage…
up the spout

Daffodil

Daffodil
You are brill... iant
You are still trumpeting
Your yellowness in my vase

I am not blasé about you
You comfort me in my hospital bed
But I wish
you were chocolates instead

Urban jungle

Friday night in the heart of the city
Flamingoes in mini skirts sit looking pretty
A parakeet is pouting, whilst adjusting her bra
causing testosterone levels to erupt at the bar
which is packed with chimps
who stand with jaws salivating

Dropping stories of friends copulating
and gorillas in dicky bows with stand-offish stances
Monitor lizards exuberant dances
Outside there's a zebra & pelican crossing
And lager-fuelled chipmunks are playfully tossing
the remains of a burger at two parrots
perched on a wall
who repeat unrepeatable insults…
then fall

A pack of hyenas are convulsing with laughter
as gibbon policemen race by chasing after
a pair of slippery eels
It's a jungle out there
Meanwhile, back in the nightclub
A stilettoed vulture
is on the lookout
for a cockatoo

Ooh it's early

10a.m.
Sunday

Body
like sludge
curtains still drawn
no-one to judge me

Lying listless
Lifeless

With limbs
of soft molten lead
With fur-coated tongue
and cotton-wool head

No movement
No saliva
No thoughts
except
Sumptuous
Scrumptious
Bed

Long-term friend

I look through an imaginary window
on the train journey of life
and on a parallel track, looking back at me

I see my long-term friend
jumping onto my carriage,
discussing marriage, parental baggage
and a girl who sends our ageing hormones
into a whirl of conversational delight

Our lives bend and twist in time
and disappear into separate tunnels
before emerging and converging in a coffee shop
where cappuccinos and cakes
fuel discussions on the repercussions
of relationships halted by signal failure

20 years down the line
and suffice to say, our alternate advice to stay
on the track leading to commitment station
has worked…

but primarily for my long-term friend and I

In bed

In the kitchen
we are wolves
On the sofa
we are slugs

Aah
but in bed
we are limpets

The beauty of skin

Black skin,white skin
Hidden out of sight skin
Liver-spotted, speckled skin
covering our hands

Butcher's skin, baker's skin
Even undertaker's skin
keeps all your organs in
and your hair from falling out

Smooth skin, rough skin
& even just enough skin
to make a plastic moulded chin
for Barbie or for Ken

Rosy cheeked baby skin
Hairy nippled saggy skin
Enough to make a foreskin
Especially for men

Sensitive and hard skin
Permanently scarred skin
The touch of a lovers skin
is hard to do without

Yes
I adore skin
even
pimply and sore skin
But tickly underarm skin
just makes me scream
and shout

I wish I didn't have armpits

Death knell for bookmarks

Facing redundancy
my leather bookmark
cried
then tried
to kick
my shiny new Kindle

The world of YouTube

Saw a skateboarder pirouette
Saw a hedgehog on a trampette
Saw a granny getting soaking wet
Saw a sausage dog in a giant baguette
Saw Susan Boyle's eyebrows

Saw Darth Vader in the Star Wars canteen
Saw Eminem bleep something obscene
Saw professor Brian Cox in D:Ream
…and hoped things could only get better

Saw the magnificent 'Evolution of Dance'
Saw Britney Spears without her pants
Saw a three-legged dog in a hypnotic trance
Saw Justin Bieber sing and prance about

Saw Lady Gaga in a coat of meat
Saw a bloke do a fart in a Buddhist retreat
Saw fish give a pedicure to someone's feet

Saw a basketball player slam dunk himself
Saw Father Christmas have a fight with an elf
Saw an overweight kitten fall off a shelf
Into the sink
And it makes me think
of Louis Armstrong
Singing
'*Wonderful World*'

Chocolate heaven

In the petrol station queue
I am General Custer
Defenceless
I am surrounded by you,
you chocolate temptresses

I look away
But I feel you rub your chocolate fingers
up and down my spine
and whisper promises
of divine intimate moments

… Just you and I

Yes, I try to ignore you
but my resistance crumbles
and I thrust you onto the counter
with abandon

I exit the petrol station,
my taste buds tingling in anticipation
of you between my lips

Home now, inside the door
The fornication begins
Take me, you say
in any way you please

I am feverish now
breathless
I undrape you in the hallway
discarding your wrapper
on the bannister rail

I pause for a second
drinking in the excitement
of the pleasure to come
My guilty conscience
glowers at me
and is cast aside

We are alone now,
and together we climb
the stairway
to chocolate heaven

Imagine a world

Imagine a world
where traffic wardens gave you tickets
to the theatre
Where doctors treated you
to Sunday lunch

Imagine a world
where burglars took your hi-fi
to the repair shop
Where tax inspectors sent you a reminder
of your wife's birthday

Imagine a world
where muggers were people
who pulled funny faces at you
Where joyriders spread nothing but joy

Yet
even if we
flip reality
and find spirituality
Some bugger
will try
to kill us
...with kindness!

Women and make up

Why bother
you look pretty
without it
I said
to the face
encased
beneath the fortress
of facial cream

Her expression
denoted an imminent scream
Okay, you win
Lets kiss
and
make up

Lightning Source UK Ltd.
Milton Keynes UK

175811UK00010B/25/P